All About Vulvas and Vaginas

A Learning About Bodies Book

DORIAN SOLOT and **MARSHALL MILLER**

illustrated by **TYLER FEDER**

Henry Holt and Company

New York

For Y & J
—D. S. & M. M.

For the kids who question and the grown-ups
who answer with honesty and care.
—T. F.

Henry Holt and Company, *Publishers since 1866*
Henry Holt® is a registered trademark of Macmillan Publishing Group, LLC
120 Broadway, New York, NY 10271 · mackids.com

Text copyright © 2024 by Dorian Solot and Marshall Miller
Illustrations copyright © 2024 by Tyler Feder
All rights reserved.

Our books may be purchased in bulk for promotional, educational,
or business use. Please contact your local bookseller or the Macmillan
Corporate and Premium Sales Department at (800) 221-7945 ext. 5442
or by email at MacmillanSpecialMarkets@macmillan.com.

Library of Congress Control Number: 2023937734

First edition, 2024
Book design by Sharismar Rodriguez
Artwork rendered digitally with Procreate and Photoshop
Printed in China by R.R. Donnelley Asia Printing Solutions Ltd.,
Dongguan City, Guangdong Province

ISBN 978-1-250-85257-1
10 9 8 7 6 5 4 3 2 1

A NOTE FOR PARENTS AND CAREGIVERS

Why this book?

Many young children find vulvas confusing or surprising. Parents are sometimes unsure how to answer their questions in a way that's accurate, age-appropriate, and understandable. Parents even debate which word to use! That's where *All About Vulvas and Vaginas* comes in.

This book recognizes that young children are seeking and deserve information beyond the mere existence of the body parts. Kids notice that vulvas and vaginas themselves are complex, with inside parts and outside parts, and they note the silences and the absences: that genitals are generally not discussed, that most dolls have no genitals, and that vulvas are missing from books about belly buttons and songs about heads, shoulders, knees, and toes. This book is the one our friends and relatives told us they were searching for to read to their young children and to validate their questions and observations.

Maybe you have a vulva. Maybe you've heard the word vagina. Maybe someone in your family has a vulva. Maybe you're curious to learn more about vulvas and vaginas. They are very interesting parts of the body!

Lots of people have vulvas! Vulvas can look a little different from each other. Vulvas are lots of different skin colors. However a vulva looks is just right for that vulva!

Vulva is the word for what you see on the outside. Teenagers and grown-ups usually have some hair on their vulva. Children don't have hair there.

The vulva has two parts that usually cover up what's underneath, kind of like two doors. There are more parts inside.

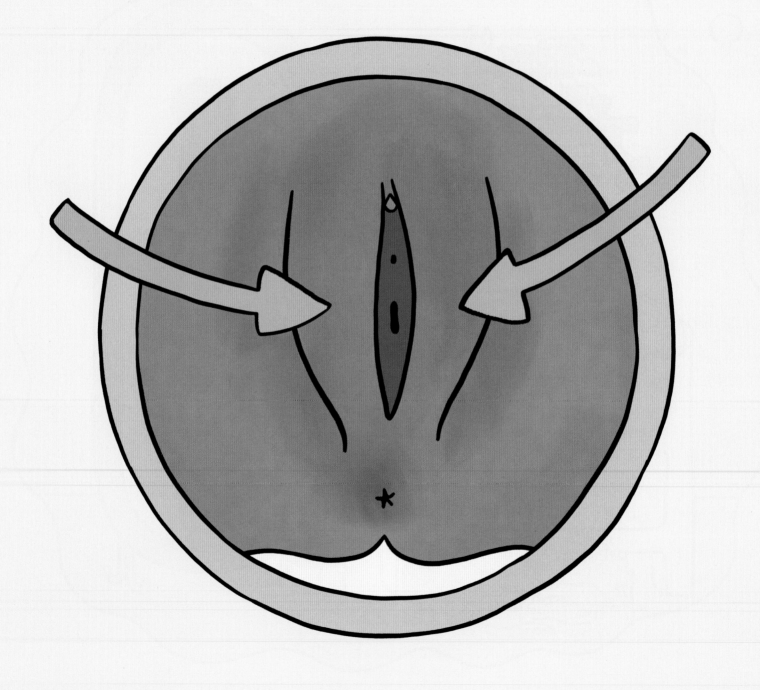

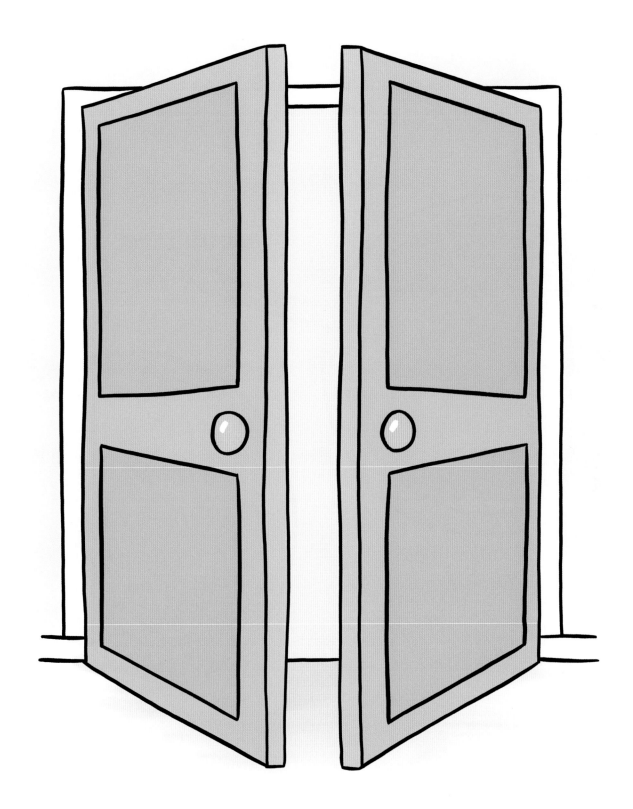

If you open up those outside parts of the vulva to peek underneath, some people have small flaps there. These parts have a special name: labia. Outer labia are the ones on the outside. Inner labia are the ones on the inside.

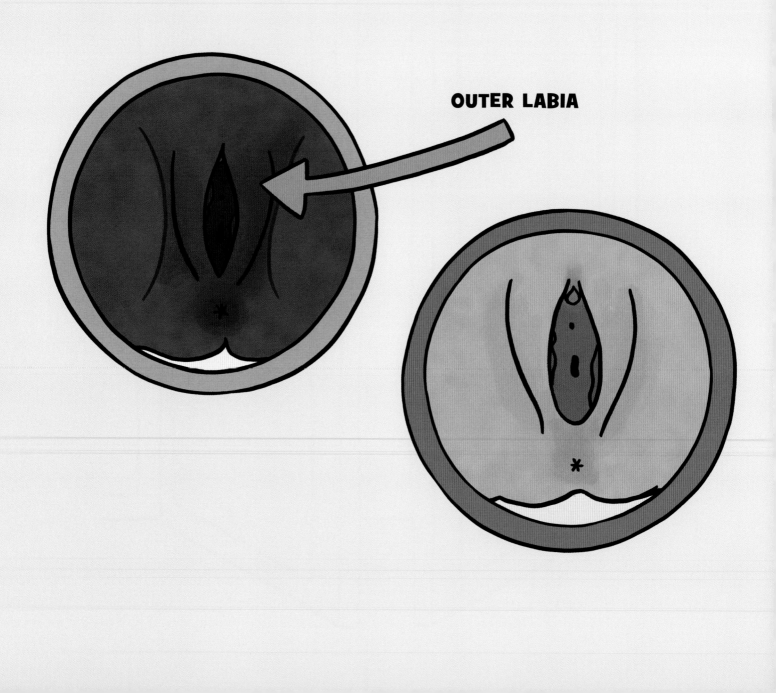

OUTER LABIA

The inside flaps can be many different sizes, shapes, and colors, or they might not be there at all. These inside flaps often grow, sometimes a little and sometimes a lot, as children grow into teenagers. However they look is just right for that body.

INNER LABIA

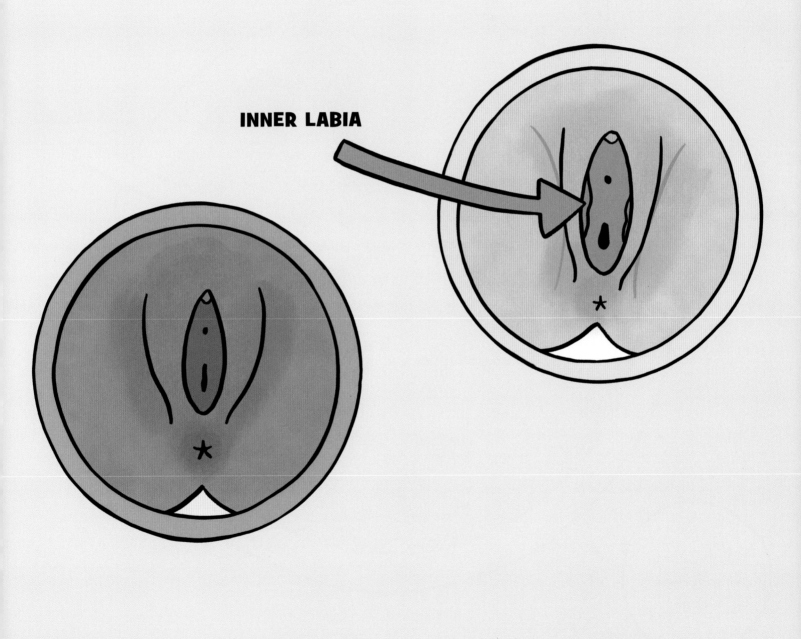

Most people who have a vulva have three holes between their legs. It can be quite a surprise to find out there are three! One hole is where pee comes out.

URETHRA

The grown-up word for pee is urine.

The name of this hole is the urethra, and it's very tiny. It can be pretty hard to see it. (The entire urethra is actually a little tube inside the body, and the hole is the opening at the very end of the tube.)

Another hole is called the vagina. This hole is the opening to another tube that's inside the body. When a grown-up has a baby, most of the time the baby is born through their vagina! Some babies are born other ways, and that's fine, too! Children's bodies aren't ready to have a baby.

PARENTS/CAREGIVERS:
For tips on explaining vaginal and cesarean birth to young children, see page 30.

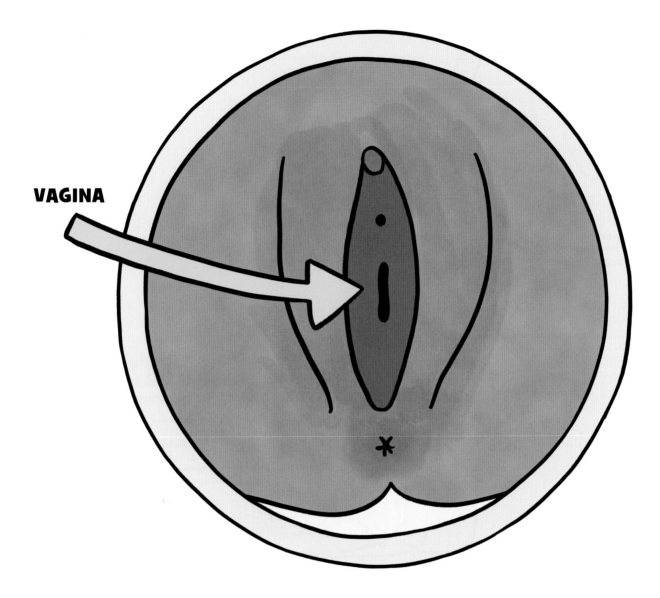

VAGINA

Some families use the word vagina when they're talking about all these parts together. That's okay, too! But if you want to be more official about it, the word vagina is the name for this opening inside the body.

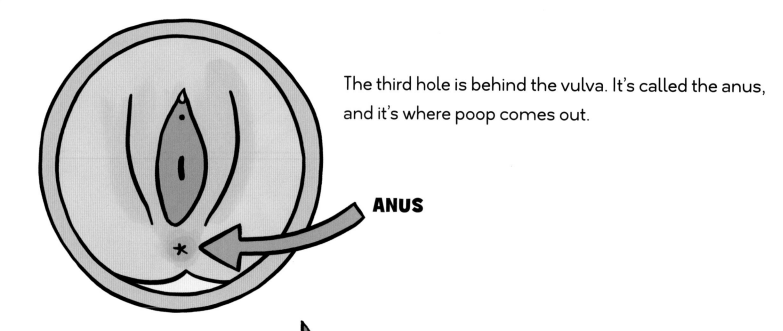

The third hole is behind the vulva. It's called the anus, and it's where poop comes out.

ANUS

CLITORIS

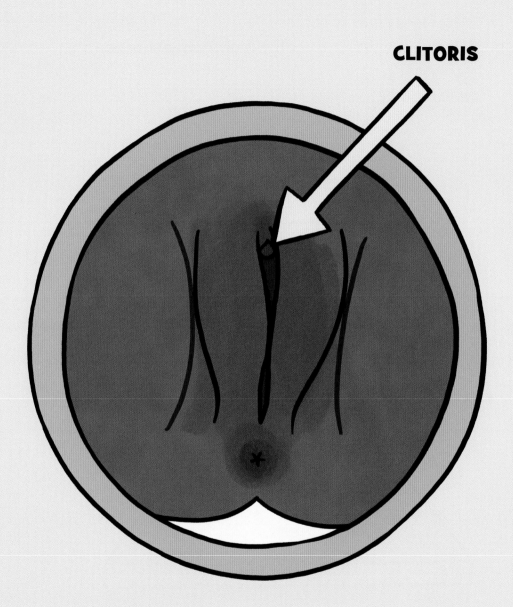

Up at the top of the vulva is a bump called the clitoris.
It has lots of nerve endings inside it.

Some people call all these parts of the body "private parts." It's okay to touch these body parts when you're in private, in a place with no other people, like in your bedroom or the bathroom at home.

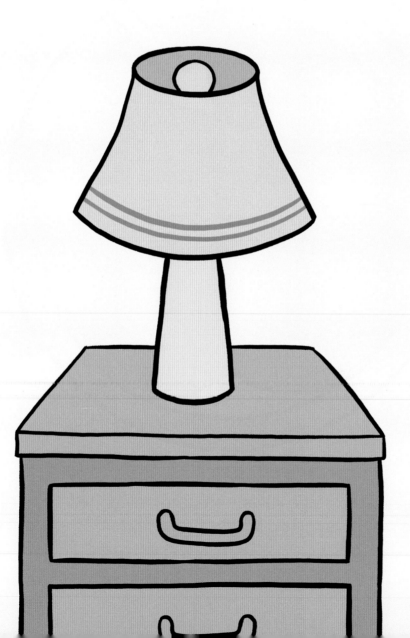

It is always okay to say no if someone else wants to touch these private parts.

It's very important not to keep touching a secret, even if someone tells you to. If you aren't sure about someone touching you or you feel mixed-up, you may decide to talk to a grown-up you trust, like a parent, a grandparent, a teacher, or a neighbor.

Vulvas and vaginas are just parts of the body, like elbows, chins, or toes. But they are also pretty special. They do things that no other body part can do.

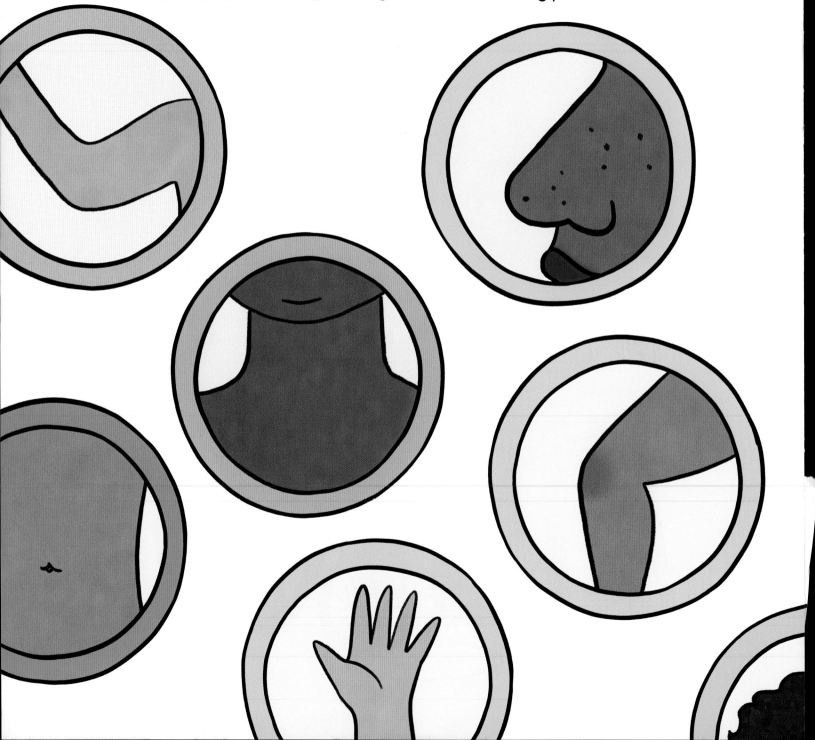

**It's good to learn
all about vulvas and vaginas!**

Additional Information for Parents and Caregivers

How to be an askable parent:

Use the correct words for body parts. Give short, honest answers to your child's questions about bodies and sexuality, then ask, "Did that answer what you wanted to know?" It's okay to say, "I need to think more about how to answer that," but follow up with an answer promptly.

Most of all, remember that one hundred 1-minute conversations about sexuality topics will make more of an impact than one 100-minute conversation. Everyday life presents constant opportunities to share your values, observations, and information with your child.

Is this book only for children with vulvas?

Definitely not! We believe it's important for all children to learn about vulvas, vaginas, and penises in all their diversity. However, we recognize that these subjects may be of interest at different times and in different contexts, which is why we created two separate books. We hope you'll also explore *All About Penises* together, if you haven't already!

About how babies are made:

While *All About Vulvas and Vaginas* touches on the idea that most babies are born from vaginas, it does not explain how babies get inside in the first place, how a newborn can fit through a hole as small as a vagina, or the concept of cesarean sections. All of these are subjects that should be explained in more detail now or later. We believe that three-to-seven-year-old children are old enough to begin to understand how babies are made and born. While some children will ask lots of questions, others never ask, in which case it's up to the parent or caregiver to start the conversation or choose a book on the subject to read together.

Since eggs are not produced from a vulva or vagina, this book does not introduce this subject. But a parent or caregiver can explain that some adults' bodies make eggs (usually, but not always, made by bodies that have a vulva) and others make sperm (usually, but not always, made by bodies that have a penis). It can be helpful to point out to children that all babies start from sperm, an egg, and a uterus where the embryo grows. And after they are born, all babies need a person or people to love and care for them. These elements can come together many different ways. The same two grown-ups may fill all the roles, or other people may be part of how a baby came to be, as in the case of adoption; surrogacy; sperm, egg, or embryo donation; or other assisted reproductive technologies.

Explaining vaginal birth:

Many children (and some adults, too!) are understandably amazed and puzzled about how a baby could be born from a small opening. It can help to explain that a grown-up's vagina is very, very strong and stretchy, a little like a balloon. It's also all wrinkled up inside, and those wrinkles can unfold to make lots more space. When it's time for a baby to be born, the vagina can stretch and the wrinkles can expand, usually very slowly, little by little, to make space for the baby to slide out. Afterward, the vagina goes back to being a small tube again, with a small opening at the end.

Explaining cesarean sections:

For a child who was born by cesarean section, or is curious about how else a baby can be born, a parent or caregiver can explain that sometimes, when it's time for a baby to be born, a doctor makes a cut in the abdomen (belly) and lifts the baby out through the cut. Then they sew the cut back up again and it heals. The doctor gives special medicine first, so the cut doesn't hurt, and being sewn back together doesn't hurt, either. Whether a baby comes out through a vagina or through the special cut called a cesarean section, they have been born! No matter how they are born, all babies need someone or some people to love them, feed them, snuggle them, and care for them.

Taking care of vulvas and vaginas:

Vaginas (the opening that leads inside the body) clean themselves, just like eyes do, and soap can actually cause problems by throwing off the healthy pH and balance of "good bacteria." Vulvas, on the other hand, are not self-cleaning and can benefit from sitting in a bathtub or rinsing with the spray from a shower. Some bodies need a finger or a washcloth to help rinse the inner area. While soap is fine for washing the outside of a vulva, it's best not to clean the inside of the vulva or inner labia with soap.

Reducing the risk of pain and itchiness:

Occasional itchiness is common and not usually a big deal. Here are some simple things you can do to reduce the risk that your child's vulva will be irritated, itchy, or painful: Use only cotton underwear and wash them with unscented laundry detergent. Teach your child how to wash the inner vulva very gently, if at all, and with only water, not soap. Perfumed and scented soaps can be especially irritating.

Why teach young children they have a clitoris, not just a vulva?

Because it is part of their body. Clitoris is not a bad word, a dirty word, or a slang word—it is simply an anatomy word. Just as we teach about the penis, including that it is okay for a child to touch their own in private, children deserve to know about the clitoris in a simple, matter-of-fact way.

About masturbation:

As any preschool or early elementary school teacher can attest, it's common for young children to discover that touching their genitals feels good. Rather than shaming children that their touching is "bad" or "dirty," parents and caregivers should redirect children matter-of-factly, teaching them that this is something to be done in private (and explaining what that word means). This book does not teach the word masturbation, but parents may choose to introduce this word.

About intersex bodies:

Not all bodies are the same! Some people are born intersex. This term means a person's body may be different from what we think of as a "girl body" or a "boy body" in terms of genitals, chromosomes, internal reproductive organs, hormone levels, or DNA. This is part of the enormous diversity of ways bodies can be.

About private parts and preventing sexual abuse:

This book takes a trauma-informed approach in how it addresses consent and the possibility of sexual abuse. Sexual abuse prevention must be primarily the responsibility of adults, not children.

Advocates now understand that the old message to "say no and tell someone right away" is unrealistic for many children and potentially harmful. Because it's common that the person who sexually abuses a child is someone they love or depend on, most children who are sexually abused are never able to say no, and many later carry tremendous guilt that they were unable to end the abuse.

It's important to emphasize to children that they are in charge of their own bodies and have the right to say no, as well as ensuring they know that being touched by someone else should never be a secret. Many children who have been sexually abused report feeling confused or mixed-up, and may feel more comfortable "asking for help" rather than "telling," since they may feel concerned about getting themselves or the other person in trouble.

Talking with kids about their bodies in age-appropriate ways can be part of helping to keep them safe. A child whose vocabulary about their body shows self-awareness is less vulnerable to anyone who is looking for children to target. Knowing body-part names could help a child be able to describe accurately what happened if abuse ever did occur. Most importantly, talking openly with your child demonstrates for them that these topics can be discussed, and that you are a person whom they can trust with their questions and concerns.

Check out the other books in this series, and also our recommendations
for other children's books on related topics, at learningaboutbodies.com.